WARM-UP EXERCISES
FOR BASS GUITAR

STRETCHES • COORDINATION EXERCISES • SCALE-BASED FINGER PATTERNS • ARPEGGIOS

By Steve Gorenberg

ISBN 978-1-4950-2996-7

HAL•LEONARD®
CORPORATION

7777 W. BLUEMOUND RD. P.O. BOX 13819 MILWAUKEE, WI 53213

In Australia Contact:
Hal Leonard Australia Pty. Ltd.
4 Lentara Court
Cheltenham, Victoria, 3192 Australia
Email: ausadmin@halleonard.com.au

Visit Hal Leonard Online at
www.halleonard.com

TABLE OF CONTENTS

INTRODUCTION

Developing a good warm-up routine is invaluable, especially for bass players, whose ability on the instrument relies a great deal on physical strength, wide stretches, and stamina. Warming up is important to the musician in the same way that it's important to athletes: it gets the blood flowing to the proper muscles and helps you to avoid cramping and risk of injury. All professional players have discovered the benefits of a good warm-up routine, especially when preparing to play long sets featuring difficult or strenuous bass lines.

An effective warm-up routine doesn't need to be played at a difficult speed or take up too much of your time. The many examples presented in *Warm-up Exercises for Bass* are suggestions for you to draw on while creating your own personal routine that will help target any specific weaknesses you'd like to work on. In the first few chapters, there are stretching exercises and simple finger patterns designed to loosen up your hands, and subsequent chapters present more scale-based exercises and musical applications. The benefits of practicing scale-based patterns is two-fold: you're getting a good warm-up and, at the same time, expanding your command of the vocabulary needed for real-world musical applications.

The best routines start slowly and progress gradually. Pay attention to what your hands are telling you. If you feel pain, stiffness, or burning, then you're probably not achieving the desired results. A good warm-up should loosen up your fingers and stretch them out, preparing you to play with comfort and ease. You'll find that many of the exercises in this book target specific fingers, certain scales and intervals, and your fretting or picking/plucking hand. As you work through the examples, make note of which ones are more difficult for you and add them to your regular routine.

Your personal warm-up program should constantly evolve, so feel free to invent your own exercises that will help to target your own specific weaknesses and improve your technique. There's nothing wrong with devoting some of your routine to improving speed, but you should always build speed gradually while warming up. Accuracy and timing are much more crucial to the bass player, so get in the habit of practicing with a metronome. Also keep in mind that there's no magic way to improve your playing by using external devices like resistance training and hand-grip gadgets. There may be some small benefit to these if you don't have your instrument readily available, but regular use of these toys can have a negative effect if they're putting a strain on the wrong muscles and tendons. Above all, keep in mind that the "no pain, no gain" approach to working out doesn't apply here. A proper warm-up routine should keep your fingers loose, keep your circulation moving, and help you to play and sound your best.

ABOUT THE AUTHOR

Steve Gorenberg is a bass player, music educator, author, arranger, transcriber, and music engraver based in Los Angeles. Steve started out at Cherry Lane Music's print division as a transcriber and in-house music editor. He has since continued as a freelance transcriber, editor, and engraver for Cherry Lane Music, *Guitar for the Practicing Musician* magazine, Hal Leonard Corp., Fred Russell Publishing, and Warner Bros. Inc., and has written, edited, and designed numerous music education products. To date, Steve has created thousands of official note-for-note guitar and bass transcriptions for artists including Metallica, Guns N' Roses, the Red Hot Chili Peppers, the Rolling Stones, Van Halen, Pearl Jam, Rush, Black Sabbath, Queen and John Mayer.

CHAPTER 1:
STRETCHING

Playing any musical instrument is a physical activity and you should get into the habit of preparing your hands and your body before you begin. A few simple stretches and routines will go a long way toward helping you loosen up and avoid injury or unnecessary straining. Just like an athlete prepares to take the field, you need to warm up those muscles and joints no matter how experienced you are. Professional players have all discovered the necessity of a good warm-up to get the blood flowing. This is especially true for the bass guitar, due to the heavy string gauges and tension, as well as the wide spacing between the frets.

Using grip devices or rubber balls to develop your muscles is not recommended. These are mostly designed to improve the grip of golfers and can end up tightening your hands and muscles rather than keeping them loose and relaxed. For this same reason, musicians are often encouraged to work out using machines instead of free weights. Although you should balance your routine and lifestyle so that it works best for you, a good rule is to pay attention to how your hands and joints feel. If you get in a good workout at the gym that leaves your hands and wrists stiff, making it uncomfortable to play, then try adjusting your routine.

A good place to start is by literally warming up your hands. Washing them in warm, soapy water helps to get your circulation flowing, and playing with fresh, clean hands will help prolong string life. It's also important to pay attention to other muscles besides the ones in your hands. Start out by doing some stretches to flex your back, shoulders, and arms. This is helpful whether you're playing standing up or sitting down. Referring to the photos below, clasp your hands together and stretch your arms high over your head and hold them in place for a few seconds. Then clasp your hands behind your back and stretch your arms backward while leaning slightly forward, holding that position for a few seconds. You should feel these stretches in your shoulders.

Now let's do some hand stretching that will loosen up your forearms, wrists, and the muscles in your palms and at the base of your fingers. Extend your arms straight out in front of you and hold your palm upward (as if you're making a "stop" motion). Use your other hand to pull back on your fingers slightly as shown in the photo below. Once you've done these stretches, turn your hand downward and pull your fingers toward you with your other hand. You should really feel this one in your forearms. Repeat these stretches for both hands.

Lastly, let do some finger stretching. Start by placing your hands together in front of you in a praying motion, but with your fingers spread apart and the fingertips of both hands touching each other. Press your fingertips and the tips of your thumbs against each other. After doing this, stretch your individual fingers one at a time by gently pressing them back with your hand as shown in the photo below.

CHAPTER 2: COORDINATION EXERCISES

This chapter contains many basic examples designed to help you warm up and stretch out those fingers. Most of the following patterns are chromatic in nature and focus on building strength and dexterity in all four fret-hand fingers, as well as improving pluck-hand coordination and precision. Since we're concentrating mostly on stretching and loosening up your fingers, speed is not essential. Choose a speed that's comfortable for you to start with and gradually build from there. It's always beneficial to practice to a metronome, no matter what the tempo is, in order to maintain consistency and improve your timing.

FRET-HAND CHROMATIC WARM-UPS

The following series of examples focuses on improving your reach and stretching your fingers by using chromatic-style patterns. Try to keep your fingers spread out across all four frets (one finger per fret), leaving your first finger anchored in place as you reach for the higher notes with your other fingers.

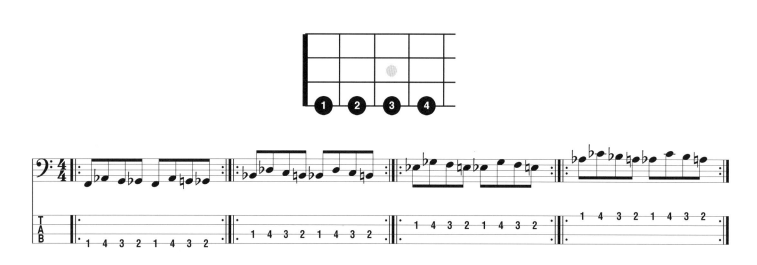

The above pattern is shown in first position (the first four frets on the bass), but it's also helpful to play the patterns in this chapter in various positions on the neck. Warm-up exercises are often played starting in first position, then repeated a fret higher each time, gradually advancing up the fretboard. Since the span between frets is much wider on the bass in first position, you might be more comfortable beginning in a higher position where the frets are closer together, then gradually moving the pattern down to the lower positions. It's not necessary to play the pattern at every fret either. Playing it in a few key positions on the fretboard should be sufficient and less tedious. Here's the same pattern, shown first at the 10th fret, then at the fifth fret:

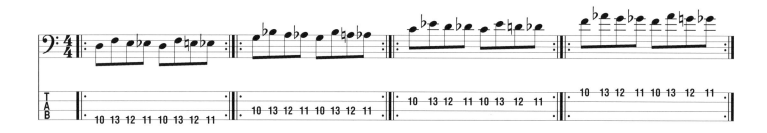

Here are four more chromatic-based patterns that switch up the order of the notes. These are all shown in first position but can be transposed and played in various other positions. Remember to try to keep your first finger anchored in place while stretching your fingers up to reach the higher notes. As with all of the exercises in this book, pay attention to what your hands are telling you physically. Pain, stiffness, or numbness in your fingers doesn't mean you're getting a good workout. Warm-up exercises are supposed to loosen your hand up and improve dexterity. If something doesn't feel right, take a break and do some stretching exercises.

This next warm-up exercise splits the chromatic pattern across two strings at a time. This is helpful to get your plucking hand accurately moving in tandem with your fret hand.

Here's the above pattern in reverse:

Now let's try that again, this time skipping over a string within the chromatic pattern. This example is a little trickier and requires more hand/eye coordination to get it flowing.

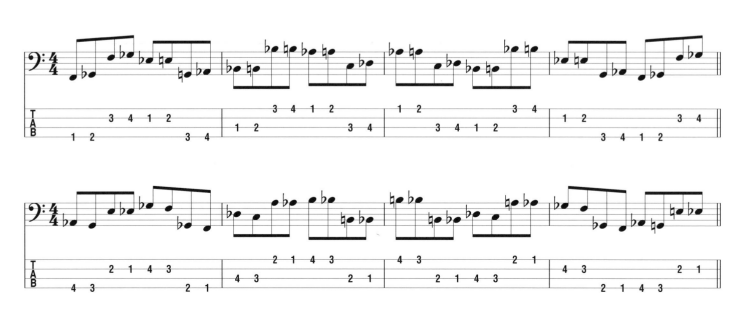

The following exercise explores every possible combination of two-finger pairings within one position on the fretboard. Play through the entire exercise continuously at first, identifying where your problem areas are located. We've shown the entire example here in the 12th position, a comfortable place to get started and that requires minimal stretching. If you can get through the whole exercise with ease, gradually move it down the fretboard, one fret at a time. The finger diagrams above each measure show you which fingers to fret the notes with.

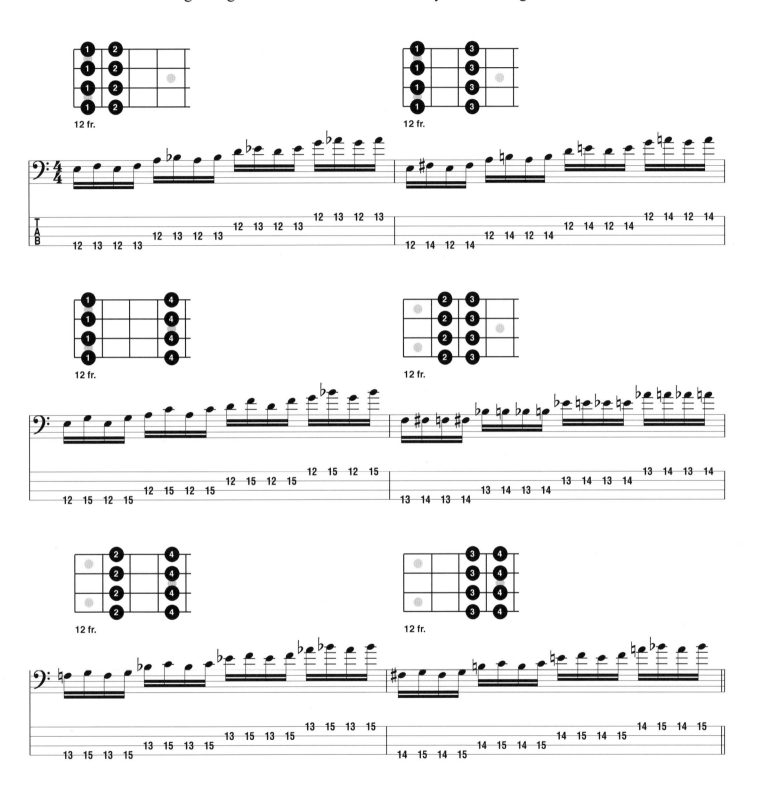

By now, you probably have a pretty good idea as to which of your fingers needs more work. If your fourth finger is weaker than the others, repeatedly play through the parts of the example that focus on strengthening it. If you're straining on the second-and-fourth-finger combination, play just that measure up and down the fretboard chromatically. Since some of these finger combinations will be more strenuous than the others, keep that in mind and avoid overdoing it. If your fingers start to burn or feel numb, take a break and shake out your hands.

PLUCK-HAND WARM-UPS

Choosing to play fingerstyle or with a pick is largely a matter of personal preference, and the exercises presented in this book can be played either way. Some bass players will alternate between fingerstyle and a pick, depending on the song and the context, but the majority of bass players tend to use one technique or the other exclusively. Despite popular belief, the main difference between fingers and a pick is the tone. A pick naturally produces a crisp, bright attack, while fingers will get you a warmer, rounded tone. Many players who solely use one technique will develop ways to approximate the tone of the other through pickups, EQ, strings, felt picks, or fingernails, but if you really want to have versatile control over your tone, it's best to be somewhat adept at both styles. You may specialize in either, but it's not unusual for a session or gig to hire someone based specifically on their playing style. That said, the argument of tone being solely attributed to a pick or fingers becomes a moot point when you consider players like Billy Sheehan or Geddy Lee—both exclusive fingerstyle players with bright, sharp attacks— or Paul McCartney—exclusively a pick player with a very warm tone.

A few myths that we can dispel at this point are that certain bass lines can only be accomplished with either a pick or fingers, or that you can play faster with a pick, or that you can only play chords with a pick. Consider the first two bass players for Metallica: Cliff Burton and Jason Newsted. Cliff was a fingerstyle player, while Jason uses a pick, yet both accomplished blistering speed and speed-metal chops. When Newsted joined Metallica following Burton's untimely death, he accomplished all of the earlier fingerstyle bass lines live with a pick. Most fingerstyle players use alternate plucking with the first and second fingers. Why would this be any different, faster or slower, than using a pick, which only has two sides? With a pick, you use an alternate down-up-down-up motion; with fingers, it's an alternate 1–2–1–2 motion. Fingerstyle players also find ways around strumming chords by using downward rake techniques with the backs of their fingernails, producing a crisper, pick-sounding tone. Since the '90s, Geddy Lee has also altered his style to basically use one finger in a back-and-forth flameco-style motion, producing a bright, pick tone with his fingernail on every other stroke. Another fallacy involves the use of three-finger plucking techniques to play faster. If you can master alternating between three plucking fingers, of course you'll be able to get more notes in faster, but tell that to Steve Harris of Iron Maiden, who has always achieved lightening speed with only two fingers. You might assume that his gallop rhythms are the result of a three-finger technique, but he has repeatedly confirmed that he only uses his index and middle fingers.

Whether you play with a pick or with your fingers, the important thing to remember is that you should strive to use alternate picking or plucking *most of the time*. Blend in economy picking when necessary, especially when skipping strings, playing arpeggios, or root-5th-octave patterns. Rather than indicating specific patterns in the following exercises, I encourage you to use common sense as your guide and see what works best for you. Start out slowly and identify places where you're not quite hitting the mark rhythmically, then correct the pluck- or pick-hand fingering to suit your own comfort and style. Keep in mind a few simple rules, like the fact that your second finger is slightly longer than your first finger and therefore gives you an advantage when reaching downward for the higher-pitched strings. Similarly, if you decide to use a three-finger technique, you'll need to angle your hand properly to balance out the length of your fingers and produce an even attack with each finger.

Here's a basic root-5th-octave pattern played at the fifth fret. Notice that this example works best using strict alternate plucking or picking.

Let's take the previous example and double up on each note, creating a 16th-note figure. It's not essential that you play this fast simply because it's presented in 16th notes; the important part is that you strive to keep a steady, even rhythm at any speed.

Here's the same root-5th-octave pattern in 16th-note triplets. Adjust your pluck-hand fingering if necessary, and be sure that you're keeping a even tempo and not hesitating when moving from string to string.

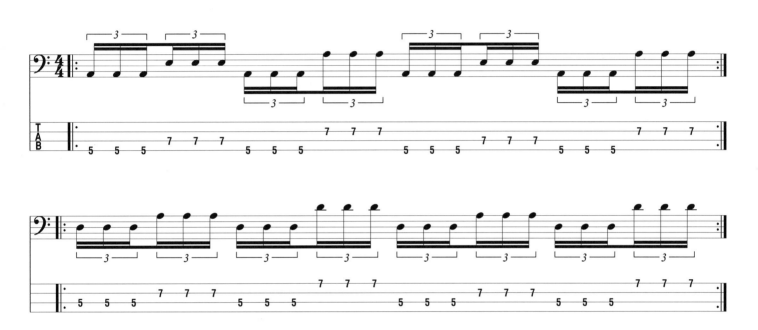

The following example features another common root-5th-octave pattern presented first as eighth notes, then 16th notes, and then 16th-note triplets.

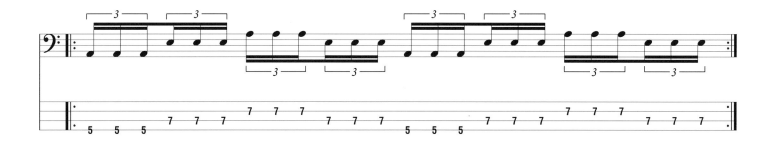

The rhythmic pattern below uses the root, 5th, and octave, and also includes the 10th for a wide, four-string stretch in the plucking hand. You'll find it necessary to use economy picking or plucking to execute this rhythm; strict alternate plucking will probably feel awkward in this case. This rhythm pattern is very popular and can be used to lock in with simple drum fills in a wide variety of musical styles.

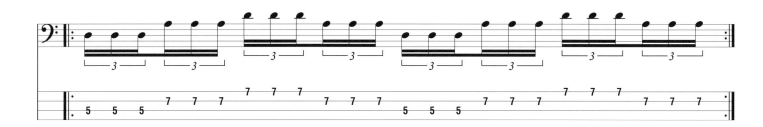

Now let's take that same rhythmic pattern and reverse the order of the notes.

Depending on the key of the song, you may find yourself playing octaves on adjacent strings, using one of the open strings for the lower note. In the following example, if you're playing fingerstyle, you'll find it easy to use strict alternate plucking, using the second finger to pluck the higher notes. This is because your second finger is longer than your first, making it more comfortable to reach the higher string.

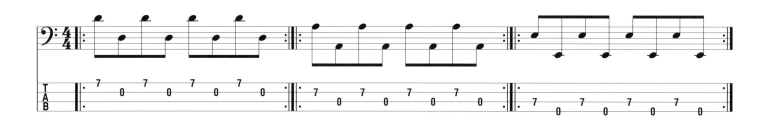

Here's a variation on the previous example, this time placing the octave on the first and third beats only. Strict alternate plucking works well with this one too, using your second finger to pluck the higher notes.

This next exercise shuffles up the rhythm to lock in with the common drum-fill pattern from the previous page. Economy plucking works well here; make sure that you're always reaching up to the higher note with your second finger.

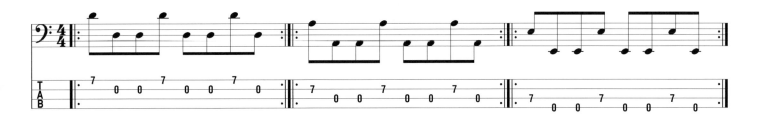

Here's one final example of the open string and octave groupings. This time, the higher octave falls on each downbeat, with the open string played twice after it, creating a series of continuous triplets.

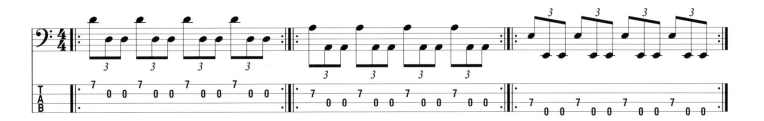

INTERVALS OF THE PENTATONIC SCALES

Pentatonic scales are the most popularly used scales for riffs and bass lines. These five-note scales are made up of two different intervals: wholes steps and minor 3rds (one-and-a-half steps). No matter which position you're in, the scale pattern will always consist of two notes per string, fretted with either the first and third fingers, the first and fourth fingers, or the second and fourth fingers. Here are the three types of finger patterns you'll encounter:

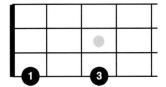 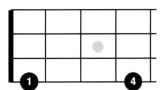 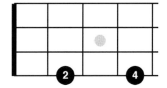

Let's play through a series of warm-ups that combine the basic pentatonic intervals in popular groupings across two adjacent strings. Remember: as with the other exercises in this chapter, we're not actually playing the scales or creating musically correct examples. These are strictly here to build finger strength while getting you used to playing common interval patterns and stretches that you'll use when playing riffs or improvising with the actual scales. We'll have plenty of warm-ups in subsequent chapters that use the pentatonics and other scales in musical applications.

The following warm-up shows a descending 3–1–3–1 finger pattern that moves chromatically up the neck and back down. This one will definitely strengthen your fingers. It's shown in notation and tab on the first and second strings, starting at the fifth fret, then progressing up to the 12th fret before changing direction and descending back down the fretboard. Play this one at a moderately fast speed and pick or pluck each note (don't use pull-offs). After playing it as written, move the pattern down to the second and third strings, then to the third and fourth strings.

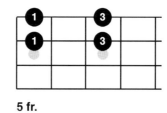

5 fr.

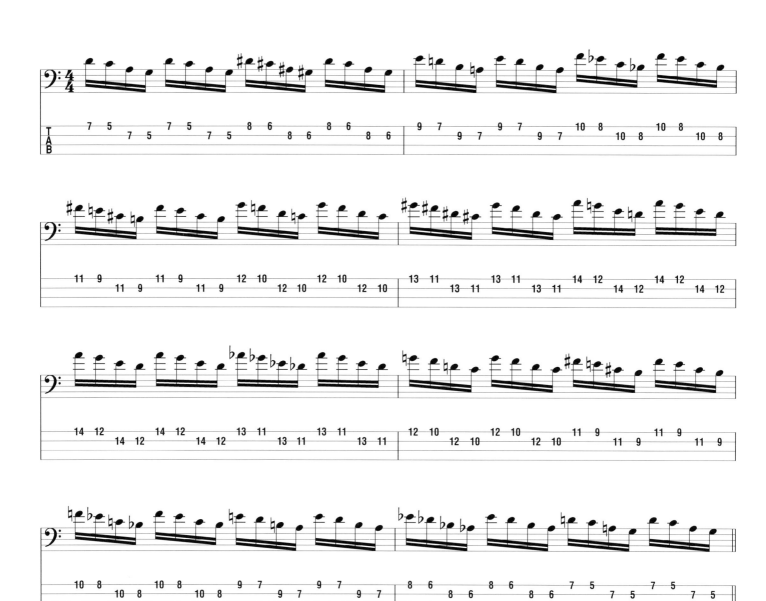

Here's a pentatonic-style pattern with a 1–4–1–3 finger pattern. Practicing this pattern as shown below will help you get your third and fourth fingers moving independently with precision.

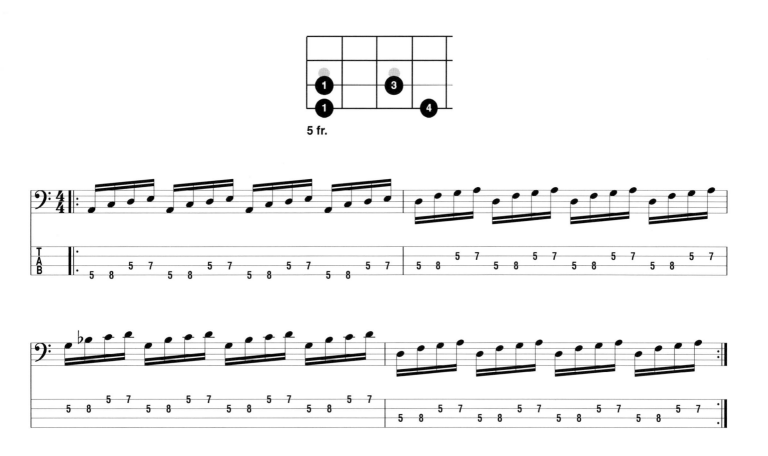

Now let's vary the above pattern, this time playing it with a 2–4–1–4 finger pattern. This one helps to strengthen independent movement in your first and second fingers.

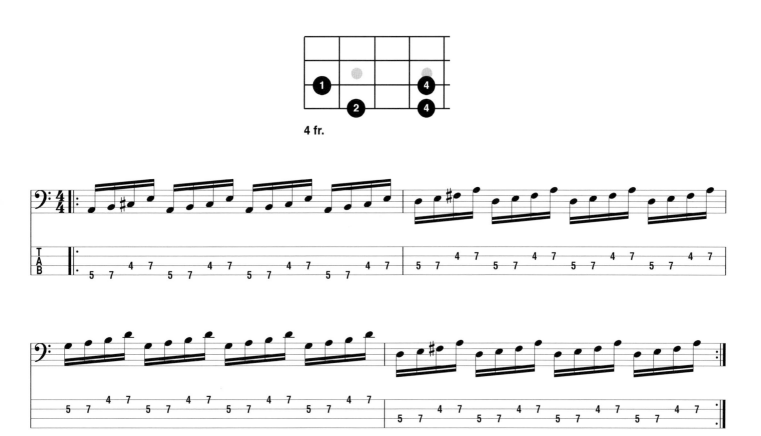

Here are a few challenging warm-ups using a 1–4–1–4 finger pattern, starting down at the first fret. These will really help strengthen your fourth finger and improve your dexterity and hand/eye coordination. The first exercise starts out on the third and fourth strings and advances the pattern two frets at a time up the fretboard and back down before repeating the pattern on the second and third strings, then on the first and second strings.

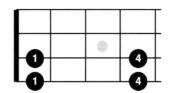

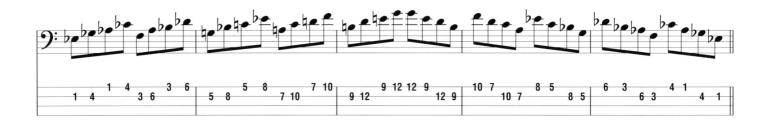

Lastly, let's take the 1–4 finger pattern and advance it up the neck one fret at a time, switching to the next adjacent string each time, as shown below. This one really helps your hand/eye coordination, as well as your left and right hand synchronization. Keep the tempo steady and make sure that you land on the right frets each time you shift positions.

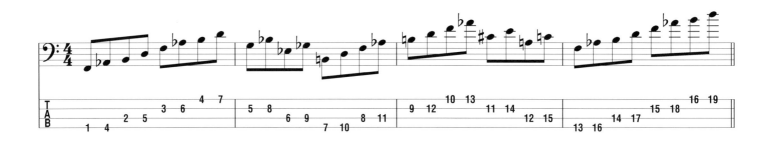

INTERVALS OF THE MAJOR AND MINOR SCALES

Major and minor scales consist of a series of half steps and whole steps. All of the positions of the scales can be played as a configuration of finger patterns that utilize three notes per string. There are only three possible finger patterns that comprise the scale positions: a whole step followed by a half step, a half step followed by a whole step, or two consecutive whole steps. Each of these finger patterns is shown below at the fifth fret:

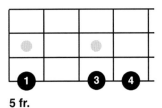
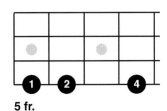
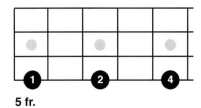

Each of the following examples uses one of the above finger patterns. These exercises are designed to get your fingers warmed up and comfortable with the stretches used to play the major and minor scales. Play each example at an even tempo, then try playing them in different areas of the fretboard.

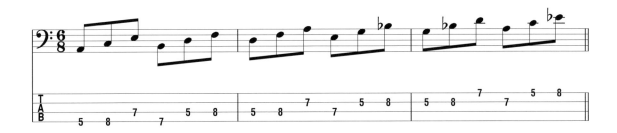

Here's a warm-up exercise that combines the three previous finger patterns. The example is presented in a triplet rhythm, advancing up the neck and back using a different finger pattern in each measure. Pluck or pick each note; don't use hammer-ons or pull-offs. Keep in mind that these examples aren't supposed to be musically correct or in any particular key; they're designed to work out your fingers with patterns and intervals that are essential to playing scales. In the following chapters, we'll present many examples that utilize these finger patterns for real-world scale applications.

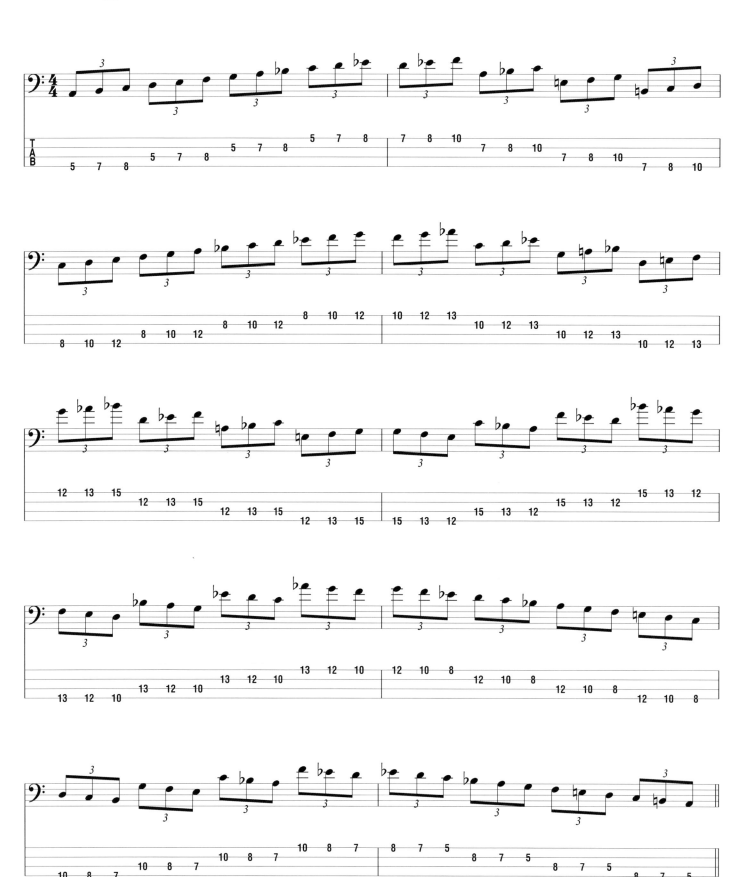

CHAPTER 3:
PENTATONIC SCALES

Pentatonic scales are five-note scales that are abbreviated versions of the regular seven-note major and minor scales. Pentatonic scales are the most commonly used scales in rock and blues music. Many bass lines and riffs are based on the pentatonic scales, and countless bass players use them exclusively to improvise bass lines.

THE A MINOR PENTATONIC SCALE

Since there are five different notes in the pentatonic scale, there are five distinct scale patterns (positions), each beginning on a different note of the scale. The first position starts with the first (root) note of the scale, the second position begins on the second note of the scale, and so on. Here are the five different scale positions for the A minor pentatonic scale, beginning with the first-position pattern, played at the fifth fret. Each pattern is shown ascending and descending in notation and tab. In the accompanying scale diagrams, the root note, A, is indicated with a white circle; all of the other notes are indicated with black circles. Play through each scale position, ascending and descending, and memorize the finger patterns.

First Position

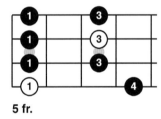

Second Position

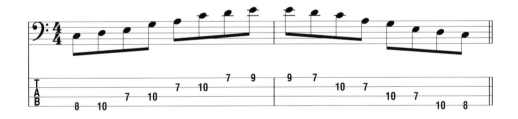
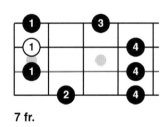

Third Position

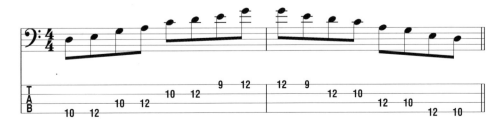
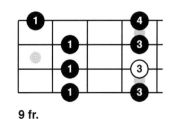

Fourth Position

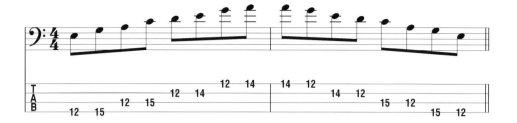

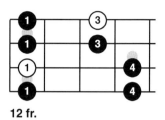

12 fr.

Fifth Position

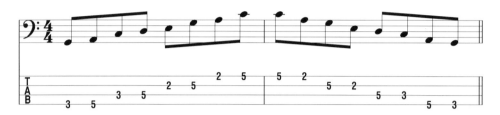

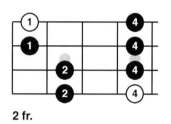

2 fr.

Depending on the context, you can use alternate fingerings to make a few of these positions more comfortable to play. When playing the third position scale pattern, you can slightly pivot your hand position by substituting your fourth finger on the second string. Try the following fingering both ascending and descending:

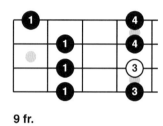

9 fr.

All of these fingerings are suggestions and you should go with what feels most comfortable to you. Of course, it isn't necessary to use the altered fingering unless you're moving between the first and second strings. Similarly, we can alter the fifth position scale like this:

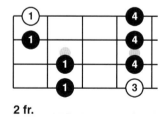

2 fr.

To give you a better sense of how these scale patterns overlap and span the entire fretboard, here's a complete fretboard diagram with the positions indicated with brackets. All of the root notes are indicated with white circles; all of the other notes are indicated with black circles.

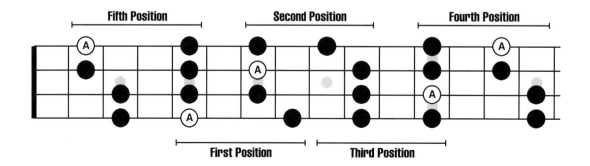

Now let's play some warm-up exercises using the A minor pentatonic scale patterns. Remember, the pentatonic scales are the most commonly used scales, so the more comfortable you are with playing the notes in different orders and patterns, the better.

The following example shows each position played in groups of three; first ascending, then descending. Try playing through all five positions as one continuous exercise. Use a metronome to ensure that you're keeping your tempo steady throughout. Once you're comfortable with the patterns and have them memorized, gradually increase your speed.

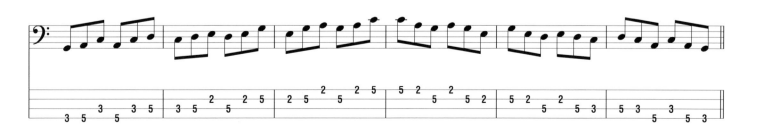

For this next example, play the notes in each scale pattern in groups of two, skipping a note each time. As before, play through all five scale patterns, ascending and descending, in one continuous exercise.

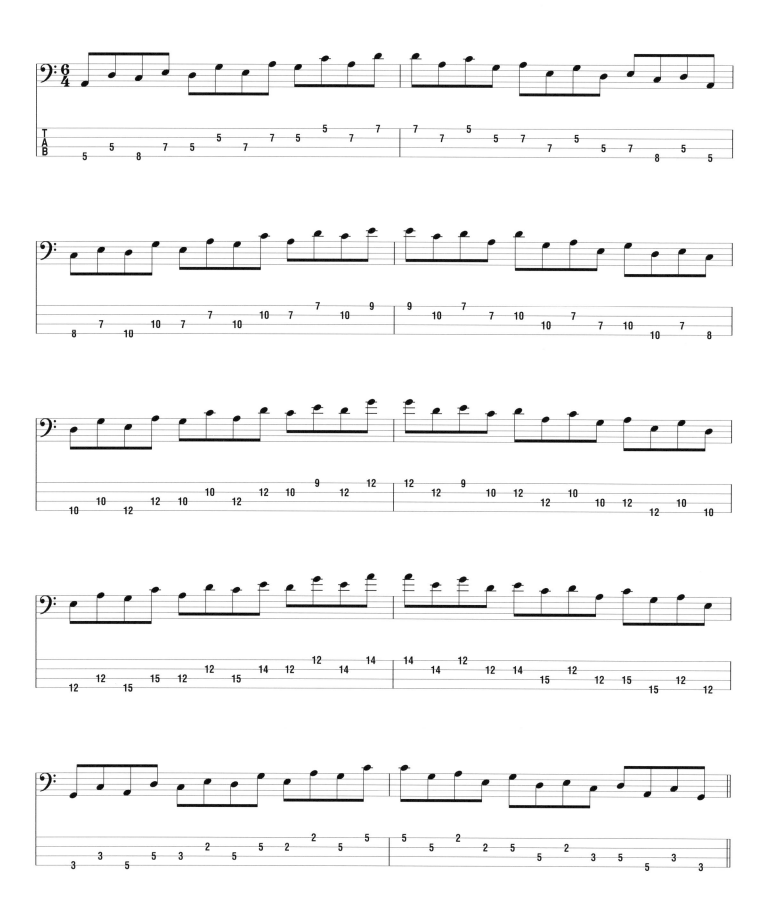

THE E MINOR PENTATONIC SCALE

Here are the minor pentatonic scale patterns in the key of E minor. Play the root notes before and after each scale position, as shown in the notation and tab. Rhythmic notation isn't used here because this is an exercise in memorization, designed to reinforce where the root notes are located in each position. This is a good exercise to apply to all of your scales, as it will improve your ability to use the scales in practical applications.

First Position

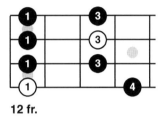

Second Position

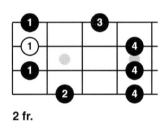

Third Position

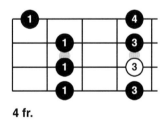

Fourth Position

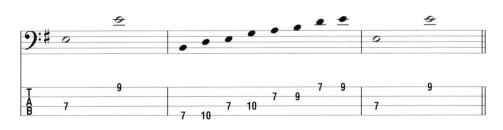
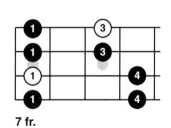

Fifth Position

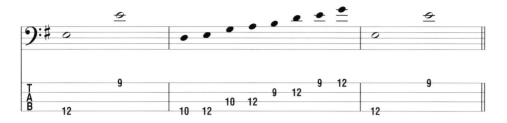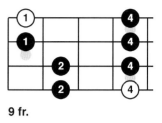

9 fr.

Now let's transpose the first-position scale pattern one octave lower to open position. There are two different scale diagram fingerings presented; both are useful for different applications. Fret the notes with your second and third fingers in situations where you might be incorporating chromatic passing tones at the first fret. Fret the notes with your first and second fingers to achieve greater speed and control when playing the "pure" pentatonic scale.

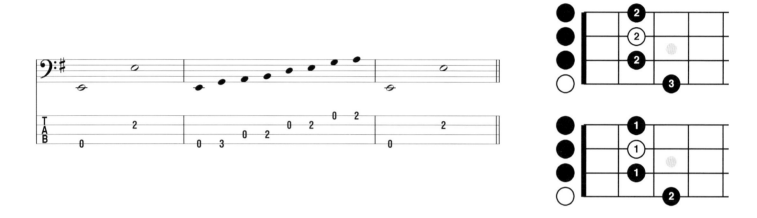

By using your first and second fingers to fret the above scale, you can combine the first- and second-position scale patterns, as shown in the following diagram. The example that follows is an exercise that incorporates both positions.

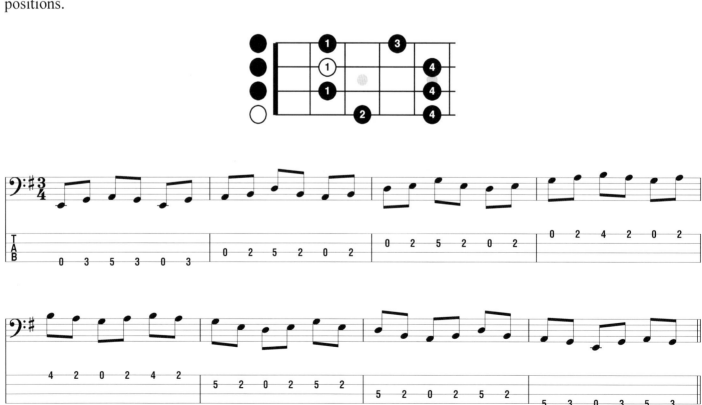

Here's a simple pattern that uses the first-position pattern of the E minor pentatonic, shown here in open position. Once you've got it down, play each of the pentatonic scale positions with the pattern.

The previous pattern can also be played using hammer-ons and pull-offs. Here it is using the fourth-position scale pattern. Use hammer-ons and pull-offs to play through all of the other positions, as well.

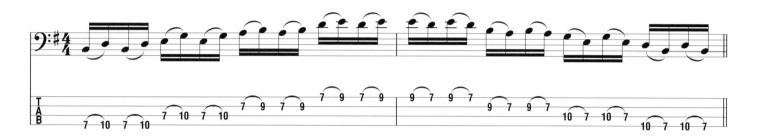

This next pattern is a bit more complex. Using a series of triplets, ascend the open-position scale pattern in the first measure, reversing the order of the triplet's notes for each subsequent string. For the next measure, descend down the second-position scale pattern, again reversing the order of the triplet's notes for each subsequent string, then progress in this fashion up the neck. This warm-up is good for hand/eye coordination and syncing up your fretting and plucking hands.

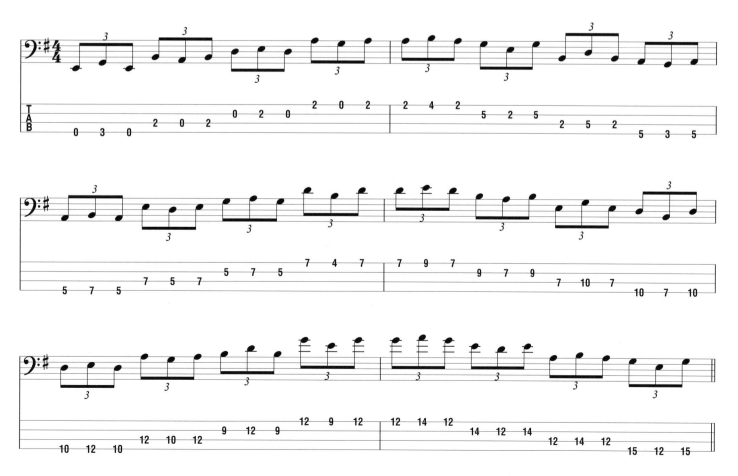

Here's a string-skipping warm-up that's good for two-hand coordination. For the first half of the exercise, each position is ascended using the notes on the fourth and second strings, then the third and first strings. Once you've reached the 12th fret, reverse the order and descend the fretboard.

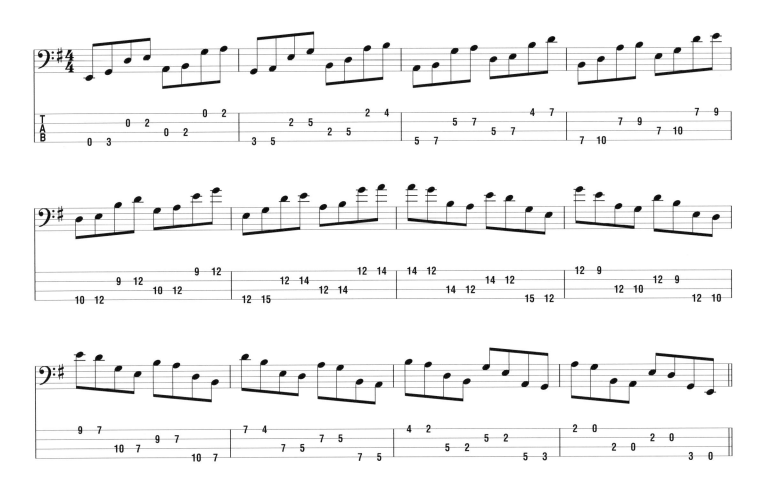

THE A MAJOR PENTATONIC SCALE

Scales that contain the same notes are called *relative scales*. Each major scale has a relative minor scale, and vice versa. Since you already know all of the scale patterns of the minor pentatonic scale, the following major pentatonic scales will look familiar; however, since they are now in a major key, the placement of the root notes in each position is different. Here are the five scale patterns for the A major pentatonic scale, starting with the first-position pattern, beginning on the root note, A, at the fifth fret of the fourth string. Play through each pattern as shown, playing the root notes in the position both before and after the scale pattern. This is a good habit to get into when practicing scales, as it will help you to memorize where all of the root notes are located on the fretboard.

First Position

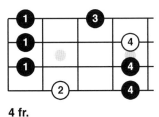

4 fr.

Second Position

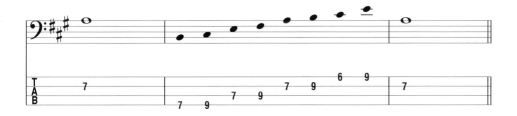

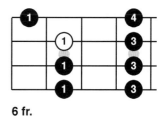

6 fr.

Third Position

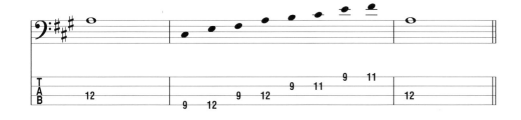

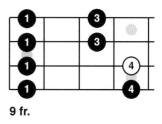

9 fr.

Fourth Position

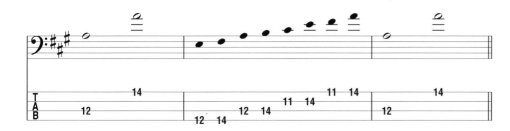

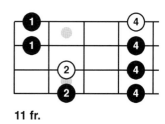

11 fr.

Fifth Position

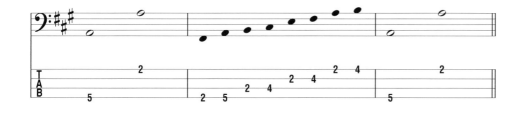

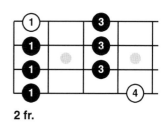

2 fr.

The following warm-up exercise uses the major pentatonic scale, starting with the fifth-position scale at the second fret of the fourth string. The pattern progresses up and down the fifth position in groups of four notes, then moves up to the first-position scale and repeats the pattern. Move up the fretboard while repeating this pattern in each position until you reach the fifth position an octave higher (the 14th fret). Keeping track of the starting note in each group of four as you play it will help you keep your place.

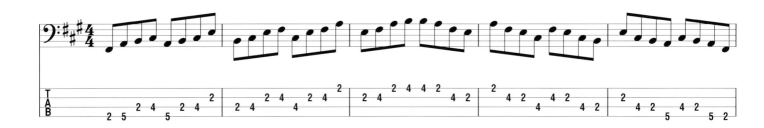

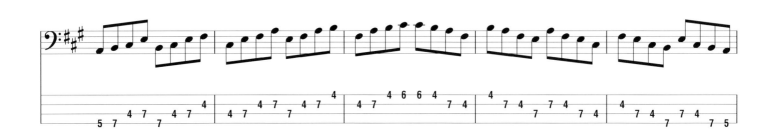

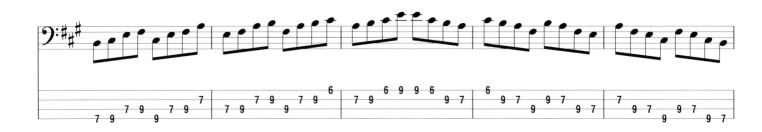

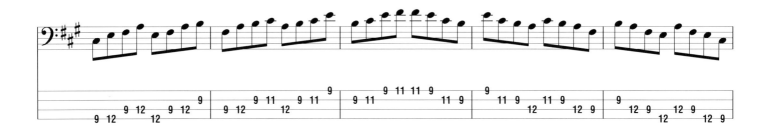

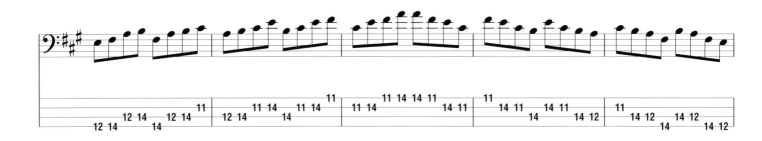

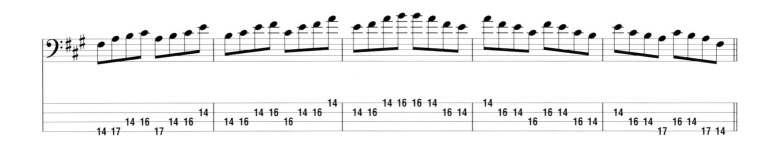

This next warm-up plays through the A major pentatonic scales in groups of five notes. Start at the second fret of the fourth string and ascend the fifth-position pattern in groups of five, then shift up to the first-position pattern and descend the notes in groups of five, progressing through the rest of the scale positions while moving up the fretboard.

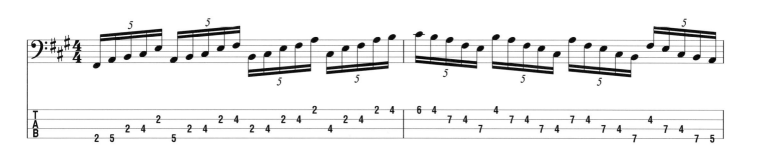

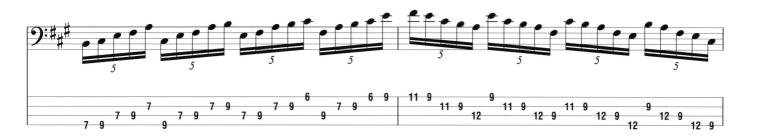

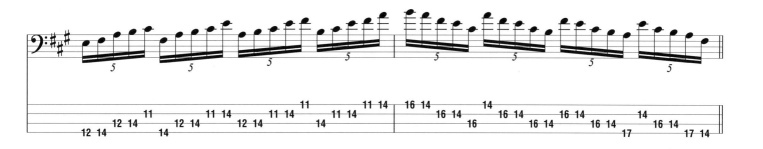

> For many warm-up exercises, accuracy is more important than speed. Your goal is to stretch and loosen up your hands. Instead of focusing on building up speed, the patterns presented in this chapter were designed to get you comfortable playing the notes of the scale in many different groupings and positions. Speed and flexibility will come naturally in time. Some of these exercises will be easier to play than others, so pinpoint your strengths and weaknesses and work on being able to play all of the warm-ups consistently.

CHAPTER 4:
MAJOR AND MINOR SCALES

In this chapter, we'll focus on the complete major and minor scales, and introduce popular patterns so that you can play the scales anywhere on the fretboard. We'll focus on a few keys and explore many warm-up exercises that you'll be able to transpose to other keys once you've got them down.

THE G MAJOR SCALE

The major scale is a seven-note scale that represents the foundation of all modern music. Even though there are seven different notes in the scale, we can use five comfortable positions to play it across the entire fretboard. Each of the following five G major scale patterns contains all of the notes that are playable in G major in that area of the fretboard. As in the previous chapter, play the root notes in each position before and after the scale to reinforce where they are located. Root notes are indicated with white circles on the scale diagrams. The second and fifth position patterns benefit from using the fourth-finger pivoting maneuver that was introduced in the previous chapter on pentatonic scales. Remember that the fingerings are not strict, and the fourth-finger pivot is only useful when you are ascending or descending in that particular part of the scale pattern. If you are improvising or playing riffs that don't require the pivot, you can easily fret those notes with your third finger instead.

First Position

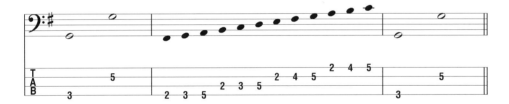
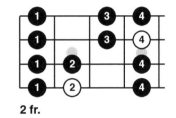

Second Position

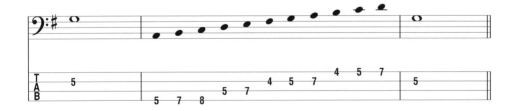
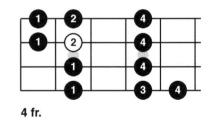

Third Position

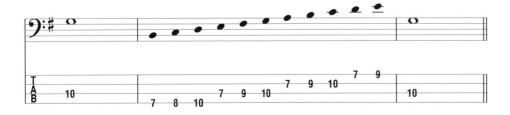
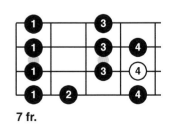

Fourth Position

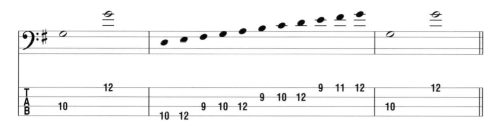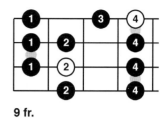

9 fr.

Fifth Position

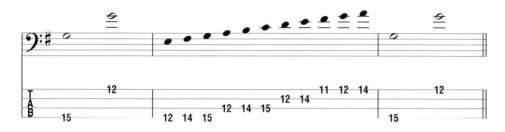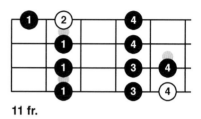

11 fr.

THE E MINOR SCALE

The E minor scale is the G major scale's relative minor, therefore both keys contain the same notes. The patterns for the scale positions are the same, but we've renumbered the positions so that the first position begins on the root note, and so on. As before, play the root notes in each position before and after playing the scale pattern to reinforce where they are located on the fretboard.

First Position

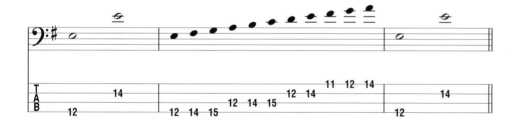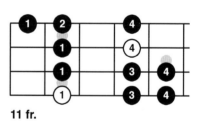

11 fr.

Second Position

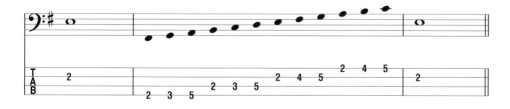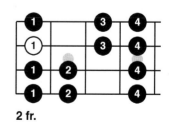

2 fr.

Third Position

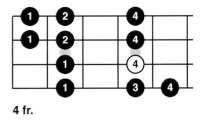

4 fr.

Fourth Position

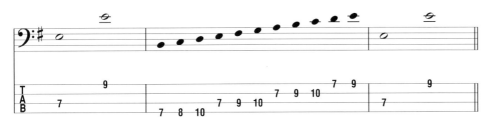
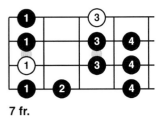

7 fr.

Fifth Position

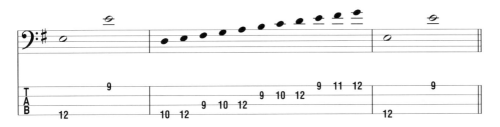
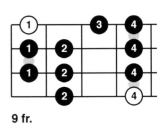

9 fr.

Since E minor is a popular key, you'll want to play the scale in open position, too. Here's the first-position scale pattern transposed one octave lower to open position:

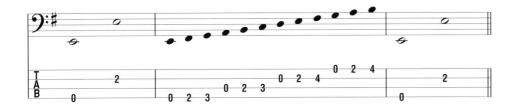
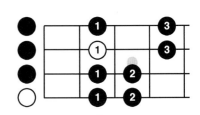

Now let's play some warm-up exercises using the G major/E minor scale patterns. This first example is shown using the first-position pattern in G major, ascending and descending the scale in 3rds. Once you've got it down, use the same pattern to play the other scale positions.

This next exercise ascends and descends the second-position G major scale pattern in groups of four. Pay attention to the places where you'll have to pivot back to the fourth fret and create a fingering that's comfortable for you. After you've got it mastered, play the other positions in groups of four notes.

Here's the open-position E minor scale played in groups of five notes. Keeping track of the first note in each grouping (on the downbeat) will help you to keep your place. This pattern may be a bit more complicated for you, but start out slow and steady and you'll pick it up in no time.

The following example plays the fifth-position E minor pattern in 4ths. The exercise is especially difficult because most of the consecutive notes occur at the same fret. This is good for improving your ability to barre across two strings on the bass with different fret-hand fingers.

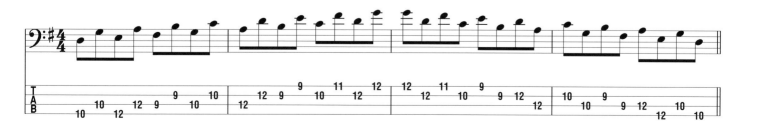

For this next exercise, ascend and descend every position of the G major scale in 6ths. Each system (line) of music focuses on a different position, starting with the first-position pattern, and progresses up the scale in 6ths as far as you can go before reversing and descending the same position. The measures are grouped in the indicated time signatures for reading convenience and to help you keep your place.

ALTERNATE FINGERINGS FOR THE G MAJOR SCALE

All of the previous major- and minor-scale patterns feature comfortable fingerings that stayed within the confines of four frets on each string. The scales can also be played using the following five alternate patterns that feature a lot of consecutive whole steps on a single string, creating wider, five-finger stretches. Each scale pattern starts on the fourth string with the first finger and contains three notes per string. Just playing these scale patterns themselves are a great warm-up exercise and will do wonders to improve your reach and strengthen the fourth finger on your fretting hand. To get the maximum benefit from playing these patterns, do your best to leave your first finger in place while stretching for the higher notes, rather than moving your whole hand to reach the notes. Playing this way helps the scale flow with a legato feel, instead of sounding choppy and cutting the notes short.

First Position

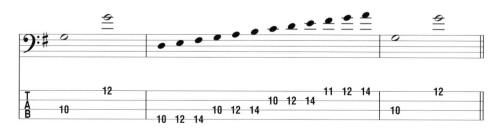

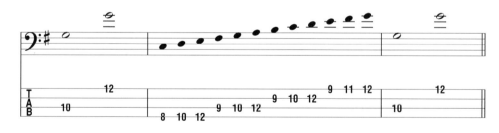

Second Position

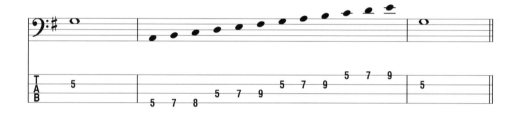

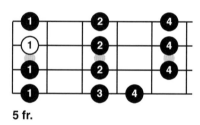

Third Position

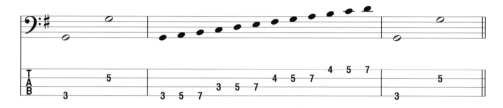

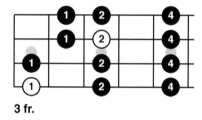

Fourth Position

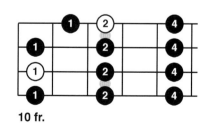

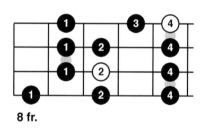

Fifth Position

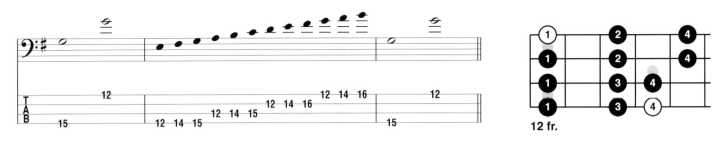

Here's a warm-up that uses the alternate major scale fingerings, played in groups of three. The first system features the first position ascending in groups of three; the second system features the same position descending. From there, the exercise goes through the rest of the positions, played in the same manner. This example is a serious workout, with a lot of intense stretching. If you can play it straight through steadily from start to finish, you'll build up some real strength and control in your fretting hand.

Developing and maintaining calluses is essential to the bass player. Naturally, you'll want good calluses built up on your fret hand, but if you're a player that plucks rather than using a pick, your pluck-hand calluses are especially important. I can't tell you how many times I've taken a vacation from regular playing for a month or two and had my calluses disappear, only to pick up the bass and, within half an hour, my fingertips are completely shredded. Plucking round-wound strings without developed calluses—especially for heavy-handed players—can create extremely painful blisters within a very short time. If you've pushed your hands to that point and you're at a gig and can't stop, you've jumped the shark and you'll end up having to bear with the agony. Blisters on your fingers are extremely painful to play with, especially if they rip open! Pluck-hand players can't do much about this; trying to tape up your fingers just doesn't work out. The best thing you can do if you've lost your calluses is prepare in advance and build them gradually over the course of a week or two. You may also try to switch to flat-wound strings temporarily, which are kinder to tender, virgin skin. Keep in mind that, once you've got some good calluses built up, all it takes is a little bit of practice every day to keep your fingers tough and ready for battle.

CHAPTER 5: ARPEGGIOS

An *arpeggio* is defined as the notes of a chord played separately. For example, a C major chord is made up of three notes: C, E, and G. If you play those three notes individually on the bass, you're playing a C major arpeggio. Knowing your arpeggios and being adept at playing them is invaluable to the bass player because they represent the notes of the chords being played by the rest of the band and will be among the best note choices when constructing bass lines.

MAJOR AND MINOR ARPEGGIOS

Let's start out with a basic C major arpeggio, consisting of the notes C, E, and G. Notice that these notes are the first, third, and fifth notes of the C major scale and are usually referred to in musical terms as the root, 3rd, and 5th. The most comfortable way to play the major arpeggio is to start out with your second finger on the root note, as shown below.

Major

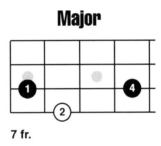

7 fr.

The following exercise begins with major arpeggios at the eighth fret; use the fingering shown in the above diagram. In the second half of the example, move the arpeggio pattern down to the third fret for an even wider stretch.

Here's the most comfortable fingering for the minor arpeggio. This is an A minor arpeggio, played at the fifth fret, starting with your first finger on the root note, A.

Minor

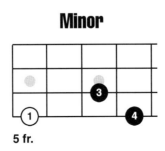

5 fr.

This next exercise is similar to the previous one and starts out with a series of minor arpeggios at the fifth fret. The second measure repeats the same minor arpeggio pattern up at the 10th fret.

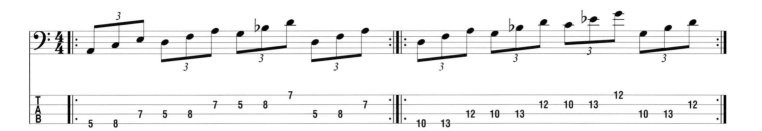

Now let's add the octave notes to each of the arpeggios. The exercise below contains a series of major arpeggios at the eighth and third frets, followed by a series of minor arpeggios at the fifth and 10th frets.

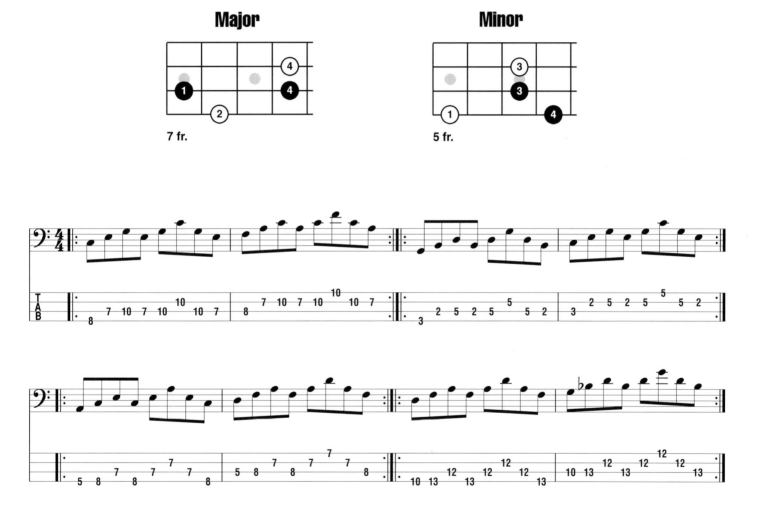

Here are a few alternate fingerings for the major and minor arpeggios; both require significant five-fret stretches. The major arpeggio starts with your first finger on the root note; the minor arpeggio starts with your second finger on the root note.

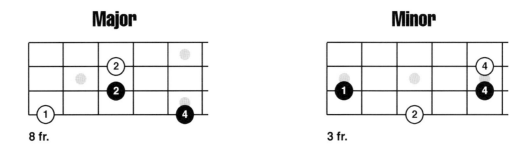

Here's a variation of the previous exercise that uses the alternate fingerings for the major and minor arpeggios. These exercises show the arpeggios in a few select areas of the fretboard, but feel free to transpose and move them to other frets.

Here are a few more fingerings for the major and minor arpeggios, both starting with your fourth finger on the root notes:

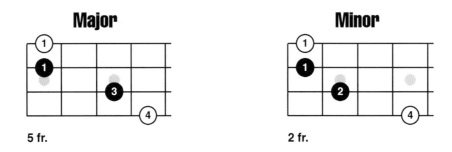

The following warm-up exercise uses the above fourth-finger arpeggios. The first system of music starts with an A major arpeggio and moves chromatically up the neck; the second system switches over to the minor arpeggio, starting at the eighth fret, then descends chromatically to the fifth fret.

We can build an arpeggio on each note of the major scale, giving us all of the chords in that particular key. The first, fourth, and fifth steps will produce major chords; the second, third, and sixth steps will produce minor chords. The seventh step of the scale produces a diminished arpeggio because it contains a flatted 5th. The chart below shows all of the chords in the key of C major.

This next warm-up exercise showcases all of the arpeggios in the key of C major, using the notes in the first-position C major scale, starting at the eighth fret of the fourth string.

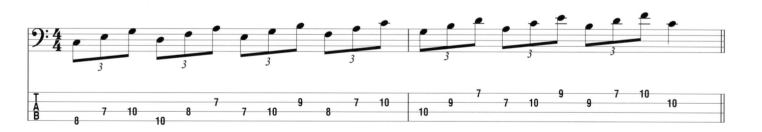

Here's a warm-up consisting of all the arpeggios in the key of G major. This one uses some of the more difficult fingerings and travels up the fretboard from G at the third fret, playing all of the arpeggios on the third and fourth strings.

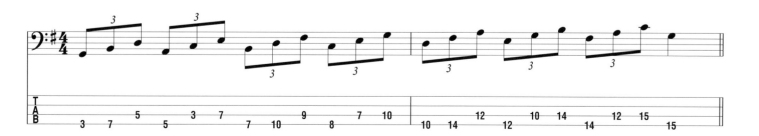

Here's a great warm-up that plays all of the arpeggios in G major, using all of the G major scale positions. The first system of music contains the arpeggios within the first-position G major scale, ascending through the scale position. Shift up to the second position scale for the second system of music and play the arpeggios in descending order. Continue this pattern until reaching the first-position scale one octave higher.

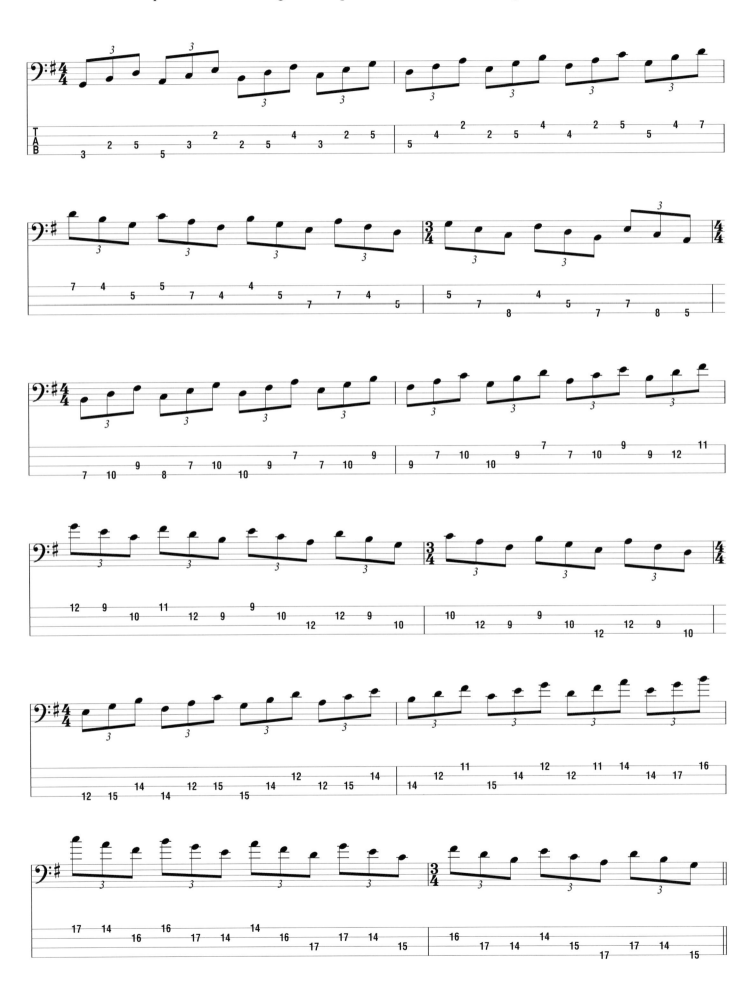

TWO-OCTAVE ARPEGGIOS

You can play two-octave arpeggios on the bass in one position by utilizing the notes on all four strings. Here are some fingerings to play the major-key arpeggios—major, minor, and diminished—across two octaves:

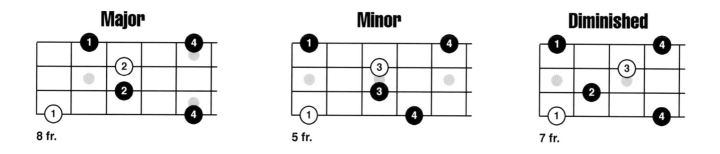

Here's an exercise that plays all of the two-octave arpeggios, ascending and descending, in the key of G major, traveling up the fretboard from G at the third fret to the octave G at the 15th fret.

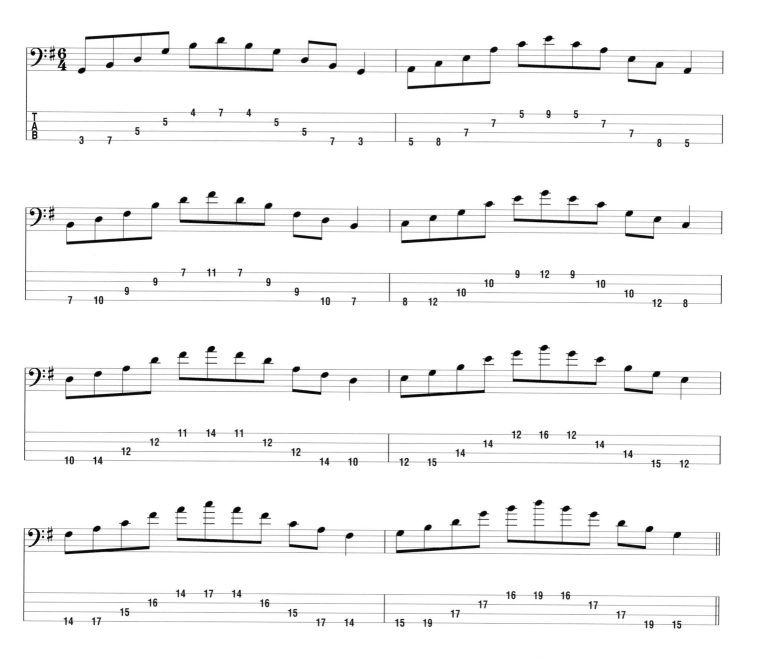

This next warm-up exercise is a variation of the previous one using the two-octave arpeggios. This example contains the arpeggios in G major traveling up the neck, ascending and descending in groups of three notes. Each system of music showcases a different arpeggio.

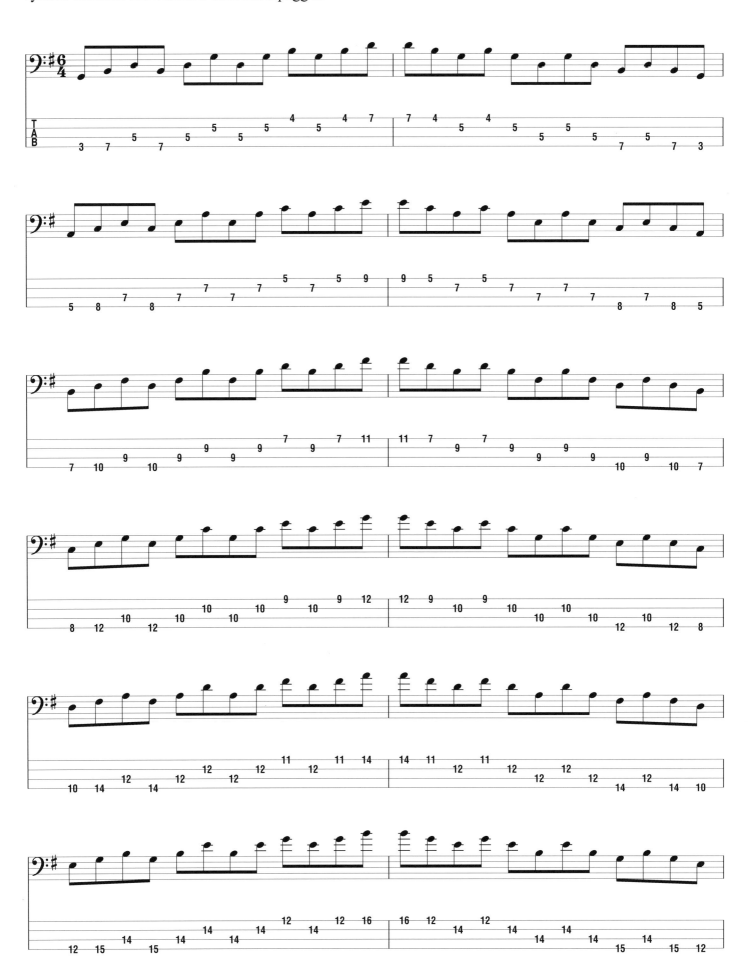

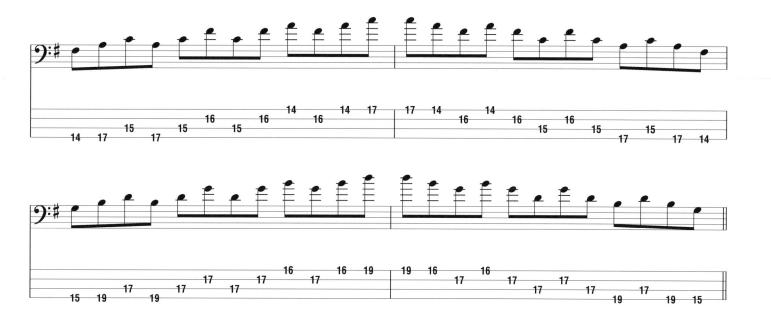

SEVENTH-CHORD ARPEGGIOS

If we extend each of the arpeggios one more chord tone, we get the seventh chords. Each step of the major scale yields a specific seventh chord. There are four types of seventh chords used in the major key: major seventh (maj7), minor seventh (m7), dominant seventh (7), and minor seventh flat-five (m7♭5).

Here are the popular fingerings for the seventh-chord arpeggios, all shown using A at the fifth fret as the root note:

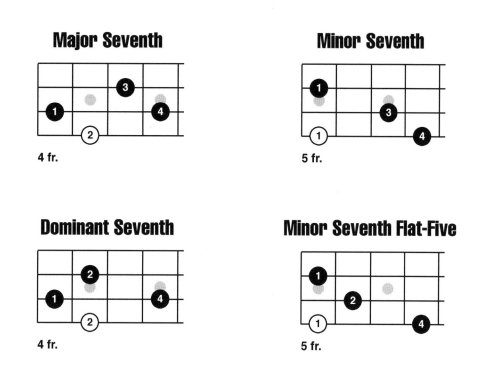

Here's a warm-up exercise that showcases all of the seventh-chord arpeggios in the key of C major, with all of the root notes played on the third string. Begin with the Cmaj7 arpeggio at the third fret and travel up the fretboard until you reach the Cmaj7 arpeggio an octave higher at the 15th fret.

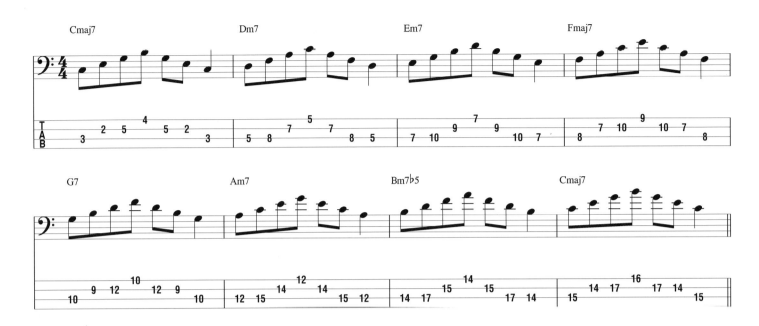

Using the same arpeggio patterns from the exercise above, here's another exercise in the key of G major, with the root notes located on the fourth string. For this example, start at the higher octave G major arpeggio at the 15th fret and work your way down the fretboard to the third fret.

DIMINISHED AND AUGMENTED ARPEGGIOS

Diminished and augmented arpeggios aren't used that often in rock and popular music, but you'll encounter them in jazz and progressive music. They're great for a workout, though, so we'll include them here and add a few more exercises.

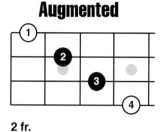

Diminished Seventh   **Augmented**

5 fr.   2 fr.

The following exercise starts at the fifth fret with the A diminished seventh arpeggio. Playing this warm-up benefits from adjusting your fingering to use a pivoting maneuver. The fingering has been indicated below the tab staff to help you along.

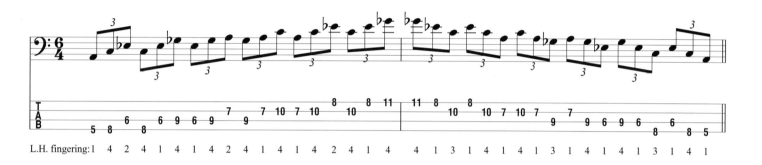

L.H. fingering: 1   4   2   4   1   4   1   4   2   4   1   4   1   4   2   4   1   4   4   1   3   1   4   1   4   1   3   1   4   1   4   1   3   1   4   1

Lastly, here's an augmented arpeggio exercise that uses all four fretting fingers and travels chromatically up the fretboard.

You can draw from all of the warm-up exercises presented in this book to create your own, personal warm-up routine. Feel free to transpose them to other keys, create your own variations, and tailor a routine that will help you to work the areas of your technique that you'd like to improve or become more comfortable with. Practicing with a metronome is invaluable, but always remember that speed is not essential and to play within your ability, without straining or over-reaching. A good warm-up will help you to loosen up your hands and muscles. Apply your routine regularly and you'll improve your stamina, helping you to avoid stiffness and injuries.

BASS BUILDERS

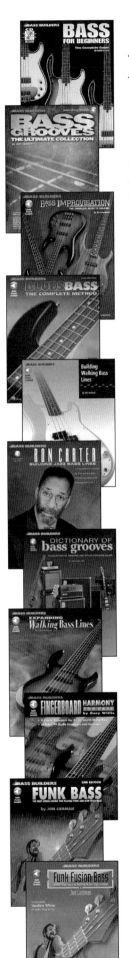

A series of technique book/audio packages created for the purposeful building and development of your chops. Each volume is written by an expert in that particular technique. And with the inclusion of audio, the added dimension of hearing exactly how to play particular grooves and techniques make these truly like private lessons.

BASS FOR BEGINNERS
by Glenn Letsch
00695099 Book/CD Pack...$19.95

BASS GROOVES
by Jon Liebman
00696028 Book/Online Audio $19.99

BASS IMPROVISATION
by Ed Friedland
00695164 Book/Online Audio $19.99

BLUES BASS
by Jon Liebman
00695235 Book/Online Audio $19.99

BUILDING WALKING BASS LINES
by Ed Friedland
00695008 Book/Online Audio $19.99

RON CARTER –
BUILDING JAZZ BASS LINES
00841240 Book/Online Audio $19.99

DICTIONARY OF BASS GROOVES
by Sean Malone
00695266 Book/Online Audio $14.95

EXPANDING WALKING BASS LINES
by Ed Friedland
00695026 Book/Online Audio $19.99

FINGERBOARD HARMONY FOR BASS
by Gary Willis
00695043 Book/Online Audio $17.99

FUNK BASS
by Jon Liebman
00699348 Book/Online Audio $19.99

FUNK/FUSION BASS
by Jon Liebman
00696553 Book/Online Audio $24.99

HIP-HOP BASS
by Josquin des Prés
00695589 Book/Online Audio $15.99

JAZZ BASS
by Ed Friedland
00695084 Book/Online Audio $17.99

JERRY JEMMOTT –
BLUES AND RHYTHM &
BLUES BASS TECHNIQUE
00695176 Book/CD Pack...$24.99

JUMP 'N' BLUES BASS
by Keith Rosier
00695292 Book/Online Audio $17.99

THE LOST ART OF COUNTRY BASS
by Keith Rosier
00695107 Book/Online Audio $19.99

PENTATONIC SCALES FOR BASS
by Ed Friedland
00696224 Book/Online Audio $19.99

REGGAE BASS
by Ed Friedland
00695163 Book/Online Audio $16.99

'70S FUNK & DISCO BASS
by Josquin des Prés
00695614 Book/Online Audio $16.99

SIMPLIFIED SIGHT-READING FOR BASS
by Josquin des Prés
00695085 Book/Online Audio $17.99

6-STRING BASSICS
by David Gross
00695221 Book/Online Audio $14.99

HAL•LEONARD®

halleonard.com

Prices, contents and availability subject to change without notice; All prices are listed in U.S. funds